FAVORITE FOOTBALL TEAMS

DALLAS COWBOYS

BY K. C. KELLEY

THE CHILD'S WORLD®

1980 Lookout Drive • Mankato, MN 56003-1705
800-599-READ • www.childsworld.com

ACKNOWLEDGMENTS

The Child's World®: Mary Berendes, Publishing Director
Shoreline Publishing Group, LLC: James Buckley, Jr., Production Director
The Design Lab: Kathleen Petelinsek, Design; Gregory Lindholm, Page Production

PHOTOS

Cover: Focus on Football
Interior: AP/Wide World: 9, 17, 18, 21; Corbis: 13; Focus on Football: 5, 6, 10,
22, 23, 25, 27; Stockexpert: 14

LIBRARY OF CONGRESS
CATALOGING-IN-PUBLICATION DATA

Kelley, K. C.
    Dallas Cowboys / by K.C. Kelley.
       p. cm. — (Favorite football teams)
    Includes bibliographical references and index.
    ISBN 978-1-60253-314-1 (library bound : alk. paper)
    1. Dallas Cowboys (Football team)—History—Juvenile literature.
I. Title. II. Series.
    GV956.D3K45 2009
    796.332'64097642812—dc22   2009009064

Printed in the United States of America
Mankato, Minnesota
November, 2009
PA02026

TABLE OF CONTENTS

Go, Cowboys!

The Dallas Cowboys all wear a big blue star on their silver helmets. That fits—the Cowboys have been big stars for a long time! They are one of the all-time best teams in the National Football League (NFL). They have won five **Super Bowls**! They have also had some of the greatest players ever. Let's take a look at this famous team!

Don't mess with the Cowboys! Here, Dallas players team up to stop the New York Giants offense from scoring a touchdown.

Who Are the Dallas Cowboys?

The Dallas Cowboys are one of 32 teams in the NFL. The NFL includes the National Football Conference (NFC) and the American Football Conference (AFC). The Cowboys play in the East Division of the NFC. The winner of the NFC plays the winner of the AFC in the Super Bowl. The Cowboys have played in eight Super Bowls.

This is where every NFL play begins—on the line of scrimmage. In this play, the Cowboys are trying to stop the New York Giants from scoring.

7

Where They Came From

The Dallas Cowboys played their first game in 1960. A pair of businessmen—Clint Murchison and Bedford Wynne—paid to start a new NFL team. They hired Tom Landry to be their coach. Landry led the team for nearly 30 years! The team started slowly, losing lots of games. By the 1970s, they were much better. They won their first Super Bowl in 1972. In 1989, Jerry Jones bought the team. Jones hired a new coach and many star players. The Cowboys won three Super Bowls in four seasons (1992-1995).

Quarterback **Roger Staubach** and coach Tom Landry were a **Super Bowl**-winning team for the Cowboys.

Who They Play

The Cowboys play 16 games each season. There are three other teams in the NFC East. They are the New York Giants, the Philadelphia Eagles, and the Washington Redskins. Every year, the Cowboys play each of those teams twice. They also play other teams in the AFC and NFC. For most of the 1970s and 1980s, the Cowboys and the Redskins were fierce **rivals**. One of these teams usually won the NFC East Division.

Dallas quarterback Tony Romo leads his team against the rival New York Giants. Romo is throwing a pass to a teammate down the field.

Where They Play

Starting in 2009, the Cowboys are playing their home games in a brand-new stadium. It's one of the biggest, fanciest, coolest stadiums around! The roof of the stadium can slide back if the day is sunny. It can close if the weather is rainy. More than 80,000 people can watch a game there. Huge TV screens hang on the outside of the stadium. The Super Bowl will be played there in 2011. Cowboys fans hope their team will be in that game!

Team owner Jerry Jones shows a model of what the new Dallas Cowboys stadium will look like. It will be the newest stadium in the NFL in 2009!

THE GAME

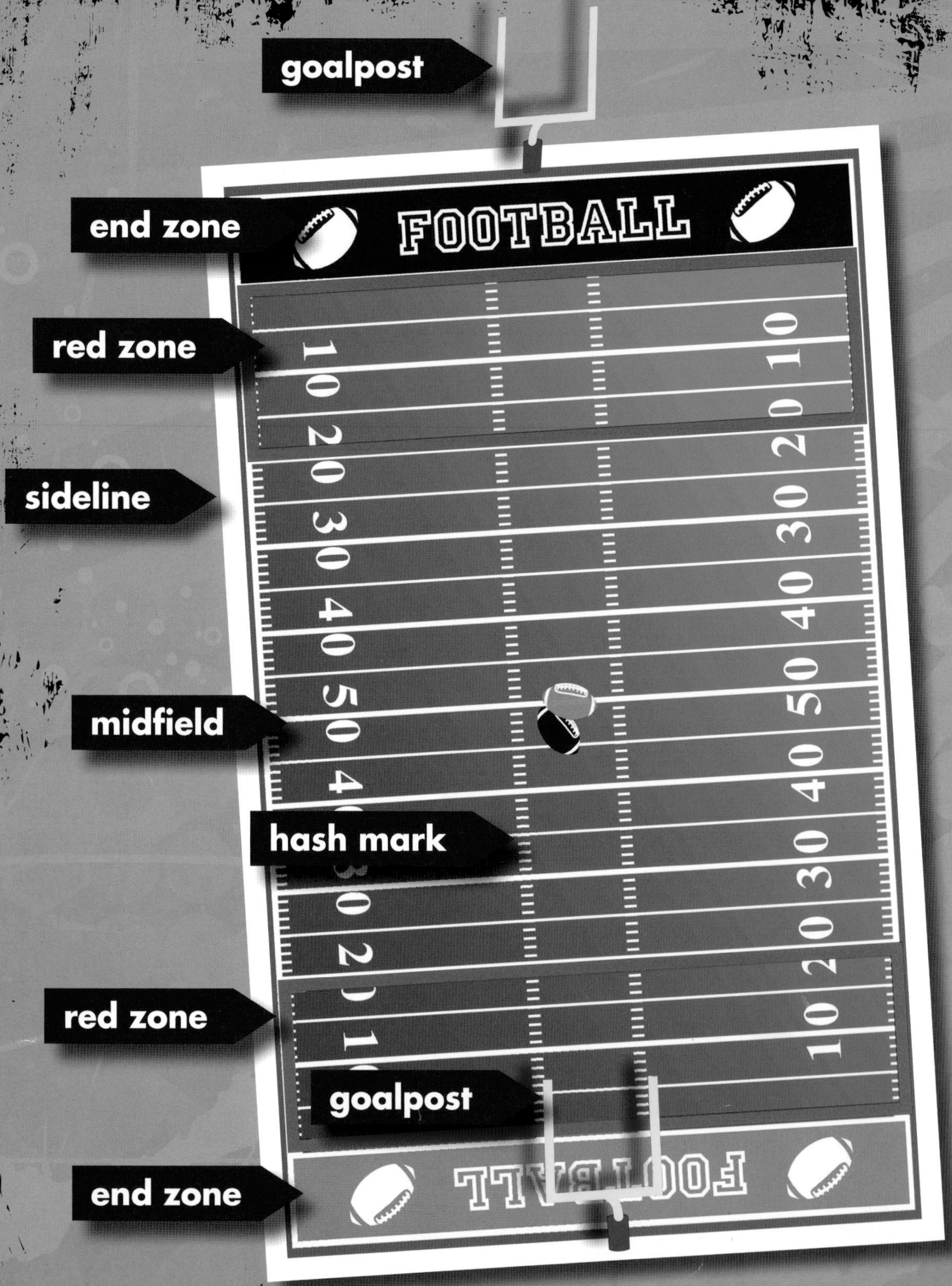

goalpost

end zone

red zone

sideline

midfield

hash mark

red zone

goalpost

end zone

FOOTBALL

10 20 30 40 50 40 30 20 10

10 20 30 40 50 40 30 20 10

FOOTBALL

The Football Field

An NFL field is 100 yards long. At each end is an **end zone** that is another 10 yards deep. Short white **hash marks** on the field mark off every yard. Longer lines mark every five yards. Numbers on the field help fans know where the players are. Goalposts stand at the back of each end zone. On some plays, a team can kick the football through the goalposts to earn points. During the game, each team stands along one sideline of the field. The Cowboys' field is covered with real grass. Some indoor NFL stadiums use **artificial**, or fake, grass.

During a game, the two teams stand on the sidelines. They usually stand near midfield, waiting for their turns to play. Coaches walk on the sidelines, too, along with cheerleaders and photographers.

15

Big Days!

The Dallas Cowboys have had many great moments in their long history. Here are three of the greatest:

1972: The team finally started playing well in the late 1960s. They ended a great run with their first Super Bowl victory over the Miami Dolphins.

1978: Dallas won their second Super Bowl. They defeated the Denver Broncos 27–10.

1996: The Cowboys won their third Super Bowl in four seasons. They beat the Pittsburgh Steelers 27–17.

Coach Tom Landry was carried off the field by his team and coaches after Super Bowl XII. Landry was famous for wearing a hat during games.

18

Tough Days!

The Cowboys can't win all their games. Some games or seasons don't turn out well. The players keep trying to play their best, though! Here are some painful memories from Cowboys history:

1979: The Cowboys lost Super Bowl XIII. Dallas's Jackie Smith dropped a sure touchdown pass in the end zone!

1989: The Cowboys had their worst season ever. They won only one of their 16 games!

2007: Quarterback Tony Romo dropped a snap on a **field goal**. If the kick had been made, Dallas would have won a playoff game.

Oh, no! Tony Romo drops the ball in a 2007 playoff game. This mistake keeps Martin Gramatica from kicking a field goal that could have won the game.

Meet the Fans

Dallas fans are very proud of their team. They wear bright blue stars on their shirts, hats, and jackets. Their team's many winning seasons have given them a lot to cheer about. Dallas is a popular team outside of Texas, too. Many people who used to live in Texas now live in other cities. These fans wait for the Cowboys to visit their new city. Then they come out to cheer . . . loudly!

This Cowboys fan got creative to cheer for his team. The goalposts on his head say "Folk Art." The Cowboys kicker is named Nick Folk!

Heroes Then . . .

Quarterback Roger Staubach was the Cowboys' first big star. He was called "Roger the Dodger." He was great at escaping tacklers. Staubach led the Cowboys to two Super Bowl wins.

Defensive tackle Bob Lilly was known as "Mr. Cowboy." He starred for the Cowboys for 14 years. Troy Aikman was another great Dallas quarterback. He used his strong passing to help Dallas win three Super Bowls.

Running back Emmitt Smith helped Aikman win games. Smith ended up with more **rushing** yards than any player in NFL history.

1989-2000

TROY AIKMAN
Quarterback

Roger Staubach served in the Navy before joining the Cowboys. He used his passing and running skills to make Dallas a winner.

23

Heroes Now . . .

Tony Romo took over as starting quarterback in 2006. He quickly became a star. He has led Dallas to the playoffs twice. **Tight end** Jason Witten is one of the best in the NFL. He plays a position that combines blocking and catching. Running back Marion Barber is tough to bring down near the goal line. On **defense**, DaMarcus Ware is the star. He has had more than 50 **sacks** over his first four seasons.

DEMARCUS WARE
Defensive End

TONY ROMO
Quarterback

JASON WITTEN
Tight End

25

Gearing Up

Dallas Cowboys players wear lots of gear to help keep them safe. They wear pads from head to toe. Check out this picture of Tony Romo and learn what NFL players wear.

The Football

NFL footballs are made of four pieces of leather. White laces help the quarterback grip and throw the ball. Inside the football is a rubber bag that holds air.

Football Fact

NFL footballs don't have white lines around them. Only college teams use footballs with those lines.

helmet

facemask

shoulder pad

chest pad

hand towel

thigh pad

knee pad

cleats

27

Sports Stats

Note: All numbers are through the 2008 season.

Touchdowns

TOUCHDOWN MAKERS

These players have scored the most touchdowns for the Cowboys.

PLAYER	TOUCHDOWNS
Emmitt Smith	164
Tony Dorsett	86

PASSING FANCY

Top Cowboys quarterbacks

PLAYER	PASSING YARDS
Troy Aikman	32,942
Roger Staubach	22,700

Quarterbacks

RUN FOR GLORY

Top Cowboys running backs

PLAYER	RUSHING YARDS
Emmitt Smith	17,162
Tony Dorsett	12,036

Running backs

28

Receivers

CATCH A STAR
Top Cowboys receivers

PLAYER	CATCHES
Michael Irvin	750
Drew Pearson	489

TOP DEFENDERS
Cowboys defensive records

Most **interceptions**: Mel Renfro, 52
Most sacks: Jim Jeffcoat, 94.5

Defenders

COACH
Most Coaching Wins

Tom Landry, 270

Coach

Index

About the Author

K. C. Kelley is a huge football fan! He has written dozens of books on football and other sports for young readers. K. C. used to work for NFL Publishing and has covered several Super Bowls.